D1465860

Poetry Art & Truth

A Picture and A Story

To: Will
Enjoy...
Artfully yours,
Gerome
09/17/04

Gerome Meminger Sr.

Art By Gerome Publishing Co.
P. O. Box 8151
Hampton, VA 23666
artbygerome@starpower.net
website: www.artbygerome.com

Cover Design by Image Typesetting & Printing
All artwork created by Gerome Meminger Sr.

First Edition January 2003

Library of Congress Control Number: 2002095946

Printed on acid free paper.
Printed In China

10 9 8 7 6 5 4 3 2 1

Photographers:
    Elizabeth Brown - Pages 15 25 31 73 77 91
    Christopher Scott - Pages 7 9 19 21 23 27 67 83 95 96
    Gerome Meminger Sr. - Pages 1 2 3 5 11 13 17 24 29 33 37 39 41 45 47 51 53 55 57 63 65 75
                    76 81 85 87 89 93 97 98 99 101 102 103 105 106 108 110 111 112 114 115

Acknowledgment

Thanks to my lovely wife Linda, for being supportive of all my dreams and the many roads I traveled to finally arrive at this place and time. Please forgive me for so many of my paintings you had to step around, as I used the entire house as an easel. I had many dreams that I tried to accomplish through others, because I saw their potential. Linda you finally told me it was time to bring out the best in me…so I thank you, and most of all…I love you.

To Joyce Meeks, my friend and partner. Thanks for all the sweat equity and believing I had a gift to share, even before I realized it. Thanks for tolerating all the one person exhibits that I put you through, and your honest critiquing of my art and poetry…I thank you.

A special thanks to Pamela Dunn and Brenda Wilson for their help and guidance in my journey as an artist. You both were there in the sun and rain especially when it counted.

Thanks to my cousin Roderick K. Terry and his company Image Typesetting and Printing of Greenville, S.C. for helping me put this book together and placing this part of my life into the reader's hands.

Many thanks to friends and family that tried and made a difference.

Thanks to all my supporters and collectors of my works. To the people who purchased my poetic bookmarkers, prints, and pieces of my original art work, again thanks for your continued support…

Finally a most humble thank you to the one that placed a gift in my soul…a dream, paper, paint, and a pen beneath my hands, and an eye to see it through. He made me possible…God.

Artfully yours,
Gerome Meminger Sr.

Contents

INTRODUCTION

In writing this book, I have tried to capture ones thoughts, and their perceptions, to put them to words.

The poems are written as truth and straight to the point. Some may sting ones feelings occasionally, but as the saying goes; " The truth sometimes hurt."

I incorporate my paintings to fit the poems I write, and for the poems, I sometimes paint a picture to go along with them. The three together commanded my title: "POETRY ART & TRUTH".

This book isn't written solely about my feelings, or me, but it is written about how one may feel and their feelings about themselves... at the time.

As you read these daily thoughts, be sure to highlight your favorite, and reflect back on them occasionally...as a pick me up...to show someone else the way...as an attitude check...or when you just plain feel good about yourself.

Hopefully you will be inspired to share what is seen and what is said to someone you care about...I did...

Gerome Meminger Sr.
Hampton, Virginia

Caged Bird 2002 Acrylic and wood on canvas board, 22" x 28"

CAGED BIRD

Encaged I still fly…

I flap my wings in anticipation…

Of my release…

For once the door opens…

My spirit too will soar...

No longer will I be…

The…**CAGED BIRD.**

1

MOTHER AND CHILD

You look for guidance…

Your mother…she is there…

You look for a strong hand…

Your mother reaches out to you…

Your bike…she taught you to ride…

Your heart gets broken…

Your mother stitches it with love…

On father's day…there are

No ties that you give…

Only flowers to the one that

Struggles so you may live…

She clears the path that you must walk…

She'll teach you her language

So you too may talk…

So walk beside her, she'll

Never leave you behind…

You have a body, heart and soul…

But your mother will be

Constantly in your mind…

*You are…***MOTHER AND CHILD.**

A Fresh Start, 2001 Acrylic and cardboard on canvas, 24"x 30"

A FRESH START

Life has many twists, turns, leaps and bounds.
Often times we travel down a road,
And come to an intersection in our lives…
And we choose…mistakes are made.
Learning from them is what counts…it's called life.
When we choose wrong, we wish for a
Second chance to…make it right…
We sometimes ask, and are given…
A FRESH START.

THAT'S FAMILY

On an occasion…

On no occasion…family is strength…

Family is support…family is there…family is love…

Get togethers turn into a party of hugs…

Greetings and most of all…love…

Kissing the youngest to the oldest…

And the ones who have trouble getting around…

The love gets louder…and louder…

Stronger…and stronger…

Being held so tight, you don't want another breath…

The smell of the old family recipes…

Last year's reunion still has the flavor on my fingers…

Friends are welcomed as brothers and sisters…

It's alright…**THAT'S FAMILY.**

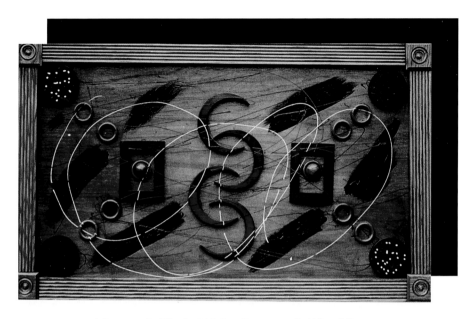

A Journey In Wood 2001 Acrylic on wood, 42" x 66"

A JOURNEY IN WOOD

To carve a path…

To carve a life…

To carve a destiny…

Often times we set out

To accomplish a task,

A goal, or acquire a dream.

Dreams come in many forms, shapes,

Sizes, and desires…carve your path with

Your biggest dreams and passions…take…

A JOURNEY IN WOOD.

DAWN

A warm glow, it's calm…relax…let your mind wander,

And drift high in the clouds on a puff of air…

A virgin breeze just passed by your senses…

You inhale, then exhale very slowly…

You are now in a state of…**DAWN.**

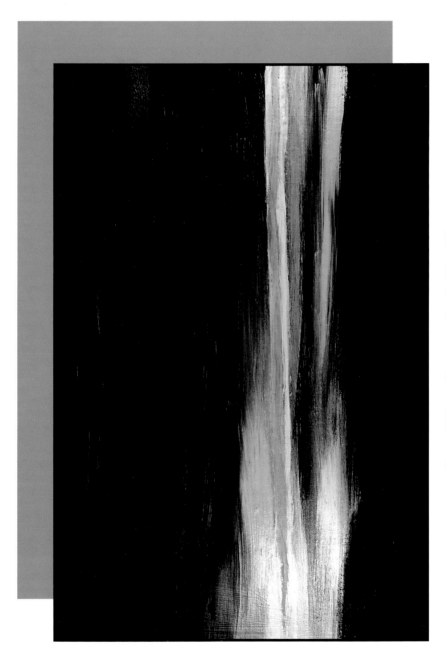

Dawn 2000 Acrylic on water board, 20" x 30"

CHALLENGE ME

A task is a task…It's no more than a task…

My size…sometimes I'm small…

Or I enjoy the food I eat, maybe…

Just one bite too many…I always did love a treat…

I may be quite taller than the average tree…

My legs…they may no longer be…

I may even be missing one of my limbs…

Like that of a tree…

The ones I arrived in the world with…

That helped to set me free…

But don't overlook the potential I have that's inside…

The potential that you can't see…

But yet I am mentally and physically able…

So…by all means…**CHALLENGE ME.**

Tiger 2000 Acrylic on water board, 20" x 30"

TIGER

Powerful...a commander...a leader...independent...

Strength comes in many forms...to be undefeated...

Able to withstand pain...self supporting...

A sole provider...a role model...all natural...

Nature at its finest...you are now the...**TIGER.**

UNAPPRECIATED SHE

He says he's hungry…
In the kitchen she prepares a meal
Fit for a king…
Served piping hot…
It's placed before him…
She waits for a smile…
He replies…can you pass me the remote…
Once again he says he's hungry…
She places before him a peanut butter sandwich…
He notices not…
UNAPPRECIATED SHE.

UNAPPRECIATED HE

She ask for a glass of water…
He prepares the most thirst quenching glass of water…
Poured in a crystal glass…he hands it to her…
She looks at it and says…it's half empty…
She asked for a glass of water again…
It is prepared in a plastic cup…this time half full…
UNAPPRECIATED HE.

Unfinished Fruit 2001 Acrylic on canvas board, 18" x 24"

UNFINISHED FRUIT

Live life, and prosper…

Often times in ones life,

We travel life's highway…

Wanting more…

Needing more…

And leaving with much less…

We wish, we dream, we hope…

For one last bite, one last taste…the last drop…

Life is…**UNFINISHED FRUIT.**

MY QUIET ROOM

Sitting in my room alone…no sounds I hear,
No one I see …I speak not…my room is quiet…
My mind holds a personal conversation
With me and we both reply.
The sounds of silence are ooh so sweet, as I
Listen for the serenity in…**MY QUIET ROOM.**

YOU DREAM ALONE

Your dreams are yours to hold on to.
Dreams are meant to be shared and
Cherished until one day they're fulfilled.
Often times, ones dreams can not be
Realized by another…
Others don't always see your dreams,
The colors, the true meaning by it all.
Dreams are not meant to be forced upon
Another. If one chooses to be a part of
Your dream and takes hold, they'll lasso
Your purple moon, and glide with you
Higher and higher.
Always remember it's your dream…
Hopefully you don't have to **DREAM ALONE…**
Pleasant dreams…

Manhood 2002 Acrylic, fabric on water paper, 18" x 22"

MANHOOD

My son, my son...
The tools you'll need to
Develop deep inside...
As a father that's my job,
That I will provide...
I will protect you,
And watch over you as you grow...
I'll guide you and then, only then...
Will I let you go...
This gift from me to you, I call...
MANHOOD.

A FRIEND I AM

A true friend…

Will come…

When you need them most…and they can

Afford to come the least…

They'll give what they have…

Even when they have not…

A FRIEND I AM.

ALL WOMAN

The nourishment of life…

Her grace has weakened many men…

Although often misunderstood by man…

She is still able to forgive…

She gives of her body and spirit…

Which should never be taken for granted…

Nothing is permanent and she too can disappear…

For she is…**ALL WOMAN.**

Woman 2000 Acrylic, fabric on water paper, 18" x 22"

AFRICAN WOMAN

The bond that can hold a family together…
The strength when her man is exhausted….
Mind strong, color unmatched…
Shades in several flavors…
She dresses to impress, for she is aware that,
She never goes unnoticed…
Oh proud, beautiful, black woman…
AFRICAN WOMAN.

IT'S OPPORTUNITY

Knock, knock…

Who's there?…

It's opportunity…

I come knocking at the strangest times…

I like catching people unprepared…

I move very swiftly…at times,

I'll see how many people I can leave behind…

And hear the standard phrase "I did not know"…

Being prepared eliminates confusion…

Misunderstand…misdirection…

If the first opportunity is missed…

The second will never be the first…

By way of mismanaged…misinformed…

Or miscommunicated…

Gather your thoughts…ideas..and goals…

And by all means…prepare…

Don't stay down…

Knock, knock…

Who's there?…

IT'S OPPORTUNITY…you got a minute?

Odd Ball Out 2001 Acrylic and ceramic on wood, 24" x 36"

ODD BALL OUT

At times I'm looked at with eyebrows raised…

Many of my actions questioned…

Dare I take the easy road…

I venture into uncharted territory…

Searching for the answers

For what the world is about…

I guess I'm the…**ODD BALL OUT.**

THE PLAN

Sometimes you snooze you lose...

Sometimes when you're wide

Awake, you still lose...

That's life...or is it **THE PLAN**...or is it the agenda?

DRIVING FORCE

I'm driven to...

I want to complete my next

Project to...

I'm tired, but I forcefully continue...to...

To...to...to...

It's strange...I don't have the answers

To...

What is this...

DRIVING FORCE.

Patches 2001 Acrylic on canvas, 24" x 32"

PATCHES

Life is color…

Life is change…from red to blue…

White to black…yellow to green…

Life is full of change…

Life is imagination…

Life is reflecting on the past…

Life is letting be…

Life is never the same…

Life is…**PATCHES.**

UNIT

Love, love, love,

People are compassionate, people are caring,

People need to be held, caressed and consoled…

Life has barriers, walls and pain…

There is a secret passage…

A light in a tunnel that awaits ones soulmate…

Someone that provides protection, comfort and love…

Now you have become a…**UNIT.**

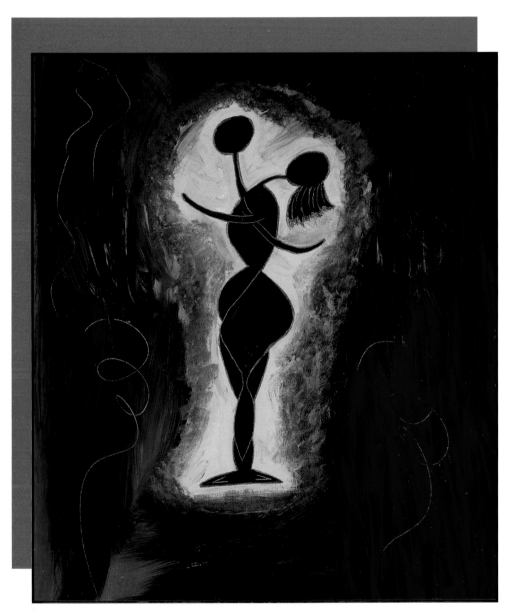

Unit 2000 Acrylic on canvas, 18" x 24"

BLACK FOREST

It's night…under a moonlit sky,

Where lies a world that speaks a special language,

Late in the wee hours…careful now…

Move very slowly and whisper quietly…

Look all around, the trees are alive…

You have wandered into the…**BLACK FOREST**

Black Forest 2000 Acrylic on water board, 20" x 30"

A Gift 2002 Acrylic on canvas board, 16" x 20"

A GIFT

To give a gift that's ooh so rare…
To have a gift, a gift to share…
To have a gift, admired by all…
To have a gift, unused will fall…
To use your gift, talent and mind…
Will lead your life to inner riches…
That one day you shall find…
We all have…**A GIFT.**

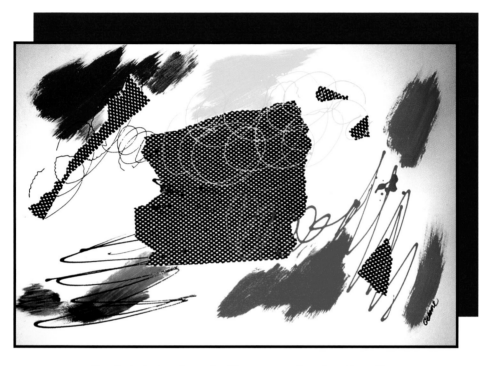

Puzzle 2001 Acrylic and rubber on water board, 20" x 30"

PUZZLE

I had it together...

I blinked my eyes and in an instant...

Someone dropped my box...

I'll gather up my life...

For this is my...

PUZZLE.

THERE'S MAGIC IN A ROSE

A rose has a magic that is

Generated out of love,

Kindness or just out

Of pure friendship.

There's magic in a rose

The red soft petals, the scent

That produces a fragrance

Of beauty, sincerity, and

A true meaning…

It's a form of love one

Can hold in one's hand,

Adore it's beauty, and

Smell it's pureness.

One can feel warm inside

Knowing life can be

Enjoyed and the rose holds love

Which is extended through it…

THERE'S MAGIC IN A ROSE.

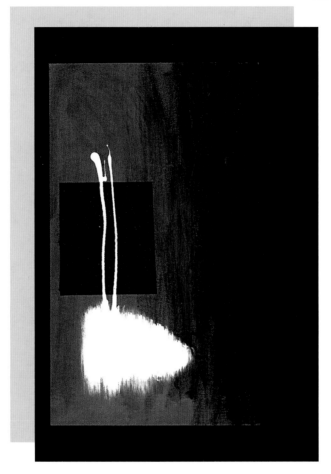

Wishbone 2001 Acrylic on water board, 20" x 30"

WISHBONE

Wishing star…you look up…make a wish that…
Your hopes and dreams may come true…
Wishing well…you looked down…
Dropped in your coins…but…
Heard no sound…don't despair…
Look straight ahead…your stomach is full…
On your plate, is left your dreams…so…
Make a wish and break in half…your…**WISHBONE.**

TWO NEW LIGHTS

Twin towers he gave to thee…
They showed prosperity, strength and
Endurance for the free.
They were symbols for
All who dreamed, had goals, and
Worked to raise their families.
He now instills a greater faith, and belief…
With two new lights
He will give to thee.
So man will continue on with hope and dignity
As we remain strong and help set others free.
Now mankind will have a clear path to see
Through the night…with this gift of…**TWO NEW LIGHTS.**

GOD DON'T PASS ME BY

The world is such a beautiful place
In which we live.
It's a shame that we have Satan as
Our neighbor…
A man is but a man, God is his
All…God don't pass me by…
In our troubles there lies only
One answer…God…
We procrastinate, but I hope It's
Just not too late.
I really want to be there, to be
A part and not left wondering
In the dark.

GOD DON'T PASS ME BY.

The Fifth Man 2002 Acrylic on water board, 20" x 30"

THE FIFTH MAN

You wanted…

You needed…

You called out…

You asked for a hand from the first man…

He said he'll see…

The second, third and fourth men had something to do…

You finally came to me as always…

I'm always there for you…even though

Our friendship is sometimes strained…

It's true and deep…

I'm known as…**THE FIFTH MAN.**

HELLO

Hello, hello…hello…

They said they would pick me

Up for work but it was 5:47…

I only have 13 minutes…

Where are they…

The cable company said they

Could only state what

Day and between the hours

Of 8am and 6pm…

It's 5pm now…hello…hello…

I loaned you what you asked for in good faith,

And now I'm being treated like a bill collector…

Hello…hello…what happen to the time

When your words meant something…

Hello…hello…operator?…

I'm sorry…the phone has been disconnected,

No further information…**HELLO!**

Man 2000 Acrylic, fabric on water paper, 18" x 22"

AFRICAN MAN

Strong, independent, a provider and protector…

Always scanning his territory…

Mind keen…wit unmatched…a warrior…

Protector of his woman, family,

And domain…strong, black man…

AFRICAN MAN.

IT'S THAT TIME OF THE YEAR

Hearts are filled with a special compassion for all...

With smiles greetings and hopes for all to be well.

What is this magic that comes and rears itself

At a certain time of the year?

Two men are playing in the sand,

What nationality is he? He has no color...

I saw Mr. Jenkins stop to give a total stranger a ride

Although no one else gets a ride in Mr. Jenkins' car.

Hearts open up without knowing why at this time of year.

It isn't questioned...the joy is just felt,

Hoping that it will last...

Maybe we should only have two months in a year...

November and December.

We'll name them, "The Magic Months".

It's that time of year...

What makes a total stranger greet you

And smile as if you've been friends yesterday

And the years before?

The world we live in is full of compassion,

Although It's mostly felt at those "magic months."

IT'S THAT TIME OF THE YEAR...*greetings.*

Women of Destiny 2002, Acrylic on canvas board, 14" x 18"

WOMEN OF DESTINY

We have love…

We have strength…

Most of all, we have faith…

Many people don't believe in miracles…however…

Women perform miracles daily as we give birth…

We are the strength…

The bond that keeps a family nourished and together…

We've fought many battles and won…

But now search for the next victory…

We pursue our goals, dreams and our passions…

We are…**WOMEN OF DESTINY.**

THE SKY

The sky…how high…
The blue color surrounding
The serenity of my above…
If I reach, may I someday touch…
May I someday feel the color,
Surrounding my face…
I now grasp, but what is it I feel…
Someday I'll know just how high…
Is…**THE SKY.**

LOOK WHAT I CAN'T DO

Look what I can do…I built the perfect house
I'm a great carpenter…
Look what I can do…
I can paint a picture you wouldn't believe…
I'm a good artist…look what I can do…
I can teach several students at one time…
I'm a skilled teacher…look what I can do…
I can win any car race out there…
I'm the best race car driver…look what I can do…
I made the NBA…I'm a great ball player…
Look what I can't do…
I can't do anything without…GOD.
LOOK WHAT I CAN'T DO.

I COULD BUT I CAN'T

I could paint a picture,

But I can't watch it dry…

I could build on my

Dreams, but I can't

Stand still and watch

Others pass me by…

I could hope with arms stretched

And hands held high…

But I can't shuffle

On my knees and

Watch eagles soar

Through the sky…

I could say I want this

Or maybe even that…

But I can't and I

Won't wait for just a

Pat on my back…I need more…

I COULD BUT I CAN'T.

HAVE YOU HEARD THE SONG BIRD?

He hums a tune,

Let's out a note,

His roar is that of a steel drum, but

With the tranquility of a nightingale.

He has a song in his heart…

A melody in his mind…

Once experienced and having tasted

This songbird's call,

You too can witness the calm before the storm.

Cages can not confine this magnificent voice,

Thunder watches in silence…

To hear the sweet tunes

That are waiting to caress and embrace

All who dare to listen.

Come one, come all

Who can withstand the

Power of voice in a song.

He has a song in his heart,

The melody is in his mind…

HAVE YOU HEARD THE SONGBIRD?

Mother and Daughter 2002 Acrylic fabric on water paper, 18" x 22"

MOTHER AND DAUGHTER

We dress alike…

We act alike…

We look very much alike…

Recipes are shared in and out of the kitchen…

About boys, about men, about becoming a woman…

We are and always will be…

MOTHER AND DAUGHTER.

JUST ONE MORE

Life is joy, life is excitement, life is dull…

Can I have just one more?…

I feel I can make time stand still…

I'll close my eyes and grit my teeth and

Years will be gone, but I'll remain with my wisdom…

I'll try again…I'll try again….Just one more…

Can I have just one more?….

Often when things are going great,

We don't want them to stop…

We often wish it could go on and on….

Just one more….

A roller coaster ride with its dips and

Curves gets your adrenaline flowing,

As your ride comes to an end, your eyes

Search for the attendant to say; "keep going"

Just one more…to live, to live, to live…

Now as I live, I'm older, the clock on the wall has

A battery, I'm hoping the battery never slows down…

JUST ONE MORE.

Sisters 2002 Acrylic, fabric on water paper, 18" x 22"

SISTERS

We shared many things…

We really cared about each other…

We cried together…

We tried different things together…

Your dress was my dress…

My shoes belong to the both of us…

We were and always will be…

SISTERS.

SHARING

A greedy person just asks for more…

An unselfish person just gives more…

And receives more to give.

While…**SHARING.**

KNOWLEDGE

Studying is like a map, showing the way,

Learning is like the streets, maps unstudied, streets unknown.

Where's your house? How can you find the streets

That you seek, which unfolds the knowledge.

Therefore the map and streets are one's

Guide to all the mysteries of the universe…

*Where's your house? Do you have the…***KNOWLEDGE.**

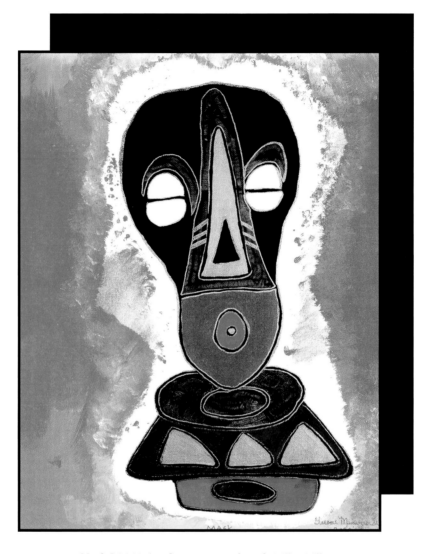

Mask I 2000 Acrylic on canvas board, 14" x 18"

MASK I

(King)

I Came…I Ruled…I Conquered.

WHO ARE WE

We met, we danced, laughed and smiled awhile…

Who are we…

The conversation was pleasant, the crowd

Seemed to disappear as the time passed.

Who are we…

We held midnight conversations that were

Lost until we meet in our minds and our

Thoughts dial our phone numbers…

Who are we…

We are distant in age but very close in mind,

We seem to be in tune with the signals

Each of us are transmitting…

Who are we…

Maybe soon we will both know…

WHO ARE WE.

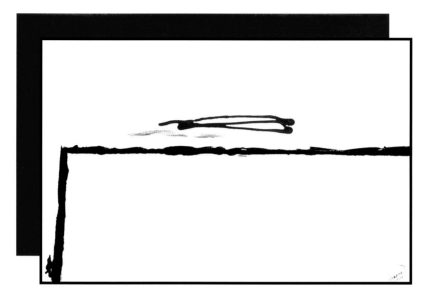

Life Line 2001, Acrylic on canvas, 30" x 40"

LIFE LINE

You arrived in this world alone…

You were nourished from a baby…

To a child…and later became an adult.

As we know, nothing lasts forever…

All of our batteries will one day slow down…

Eventually come to a halt…

Don't worry, because of the love that I have for you…

I will *gladly be your*…**LIFE LINE.**

JUMPING TO A CONCLUSION

Jumping to conclusions have cost many friendships…

Many relationships…many futures…

If it takes several years to develop…

Why does it take just an instance…

One perception…

One misunderstanding…

To destroy them all by…

JUMPING TO A CONCLUSION.

IT'S TIME TO GO HOME

I sat, talked, thought, and laughed

All by myself…

Many questions I asked, I also

Answered for myself…

I played a game in my mind,

It's time I played with someone else…

I sang a song…I sang it to myself…

It's time I sang it to someone I love.

I cried, I cried alone, it's time for someone

To wipe my tears away…

It's time…**IT'S TIME FOR ME TO GO HOME.**

Chain Reaction 2001 Acrylic on canvas, 24" x 60"

CHAIN REACTION

For every action…there is a chain reaction…

If something is done, it effects us all…

A ripple in a pond grows ever wider and farther…

One communicates to another and another and finally

The message gets to all…then laughter, as if it was

A joke that was told…or cries if there was sorrow

In the story…a woman has a baby…

Now the baby has a mother,

A father, maybe a sister, brother,

Aunt, uncle, grands…even…

A new world…a new frontier, a friend..

For every action there is always…a **CHAIN REACTION.**

THE CHAMBERS OF MY MIND

Dreams filled the chambers of my mind.

My destiny often wonders…directions,

Problems, solutions would fill the

Chambers of my mind.

Patience is a virtue, often learned, one

Of life's lessons, not as easy for many

To grasp…questions fill the

Chambers of my mind.

Quotes, phrases, sayings are etched

In my mind. I search books, papers

And others.

Searching for all world answers, for

Many solutions, are filled in…

THE CHAMBERS OF MY MIND.

Old Wise One 2002 Acrylic on canvas, 32" x 32"

OLD WISE ONE

Sunshine cast its shadow down on a tree…
Its radiant glare sometimes cast a shadow down on me…
If you look hard enough at an isolated tree,
It can tell a story about how things used to be…
Many stories…locked inside…peel the bark
And with a polite request…ask your questions
and listen closely…for the answers to life's test…
As the sun sets on the limbs…a prayer is said by many…
By some…tomorrow the limbs…they may not stretch…
They may not fold their arms…and head too is bent…
Cherish the tree…no more answers…
It is now heaven sent…
Cherish the…**OLD WISE ONE**…
Time well spent.

A *SYMBOL* OF INNOCENCE

In a crystal vase are stems, and at

The ends I see beautiful flowers

With soft white petals. If I touch may

I one day be…

A symbol of innocence…

Doves fly, they fly high and float

On a puff of air, spread their wings

And smile, for they too are…

A symbol of innocence…

I hear the cry of a little baby,

The laughter of a small child…

A pure white cloud drifting high above

My beyond…the tears from a man

Who's not suppose to cry…he too

Can become…**A SYMBOL OF INNOCENCE.**

Clouds 2000 Acrylic on canvas, 20" x 30"

WALKING ON THE CLOUDS

As I fly across the open skies, clouds are

At my feet…on my left and right.

I wonder…can I walk on the clouds?

Those white puffs of mountains are

Like that of a world which comes to life

Only when viewed not from below but from above.

While soaring up in my silver dome,

I can become the ruler of that unclaimed

World below me…can I walk on the clouds?

They seem so innocent, pure and calm.

However they seem to drift keeping their own time.

One day I may step from my big

Silver dome and begin…**WALKING ON THE CLOUDS.**

WHAT ABOUT TODAY?

Tomorrow…tomorrow…next week…

Let's get together tomorrow…

I'll plan that tomorrow…

Come by next week…

Tomorrow is a space in time

Never promised for anyone's

Eyes to see…

One person, one space…

One space…one lifetime…

Your life began again today…

Maybe just for another minute…

Or an hour or two…

WHAT ABOUT TODAY?

Mask III 2000 Acrylic on water paper, 12" x 16"

MASK III

(Knowledge)

Knowledge is power...

Knowledge is power...

Knowledge makes one powerful...

IT WAS THE DARK SIDE OF THE MOONLIGHT

People, places, things, get lit up by the glow of the moonlight.

It casts it's rays of vision just for people to see,

Places to be found.

While on my journey to explore the wonders of the

World, I'm smiling, shaking hands, and complementing

My fellow man…but I hear whispers…

It was the dark side of the moonlight…

Now as I walk the streets, my paces are faster,

My head turns side to side, I feel like running…

Be still my heart…the moon is shining bright, but…

It was the dark side of the moonlight.

Now I see, I must plot my path carefully,

So that I too may see the world eye to eye.

I too have a precious world, but I feel a strange hand

In my left pocket, while softly being stroked in

The middle of my back.

The moon is shining bright, but…

IT WAS THE DARK SIDE OF THE MOONLIGHT.

Strolling 2001 Acrylic on canvas board, 14" x 18"

STROLLING

Mind free, nothing around me…

I just feel like strolling…

No bags, no papers, no communications…

I just feel like strolling…

Head clear, no worries surround me…

For I am just…**STROLLING.**

HOW FAR IS THAT

I look out of my window at a distance
As far as my eyes and imagination can
See...I then wonder...
How far is that...
I have dreams of all sizes, colors and shapes.
What will I be tomorrow? Where will I
Be tomorrow? Will I see tomorrow?
How far is that...
What's over there? If I journey to that
Distant place will I be there, or once
Again at my beginning...when do I reach
The end...
How far is that...
My tomorrow may be my today,
Who's to say? I can't find an authority
For my destiny. Perhaps I should take life
One step at a time.
I'm looking at a distance...
Am I at the beginning or at my end?
Maybe life is one big circle where
At some point you get to see yourself
From a distance...
HOW FAR IS THAT.

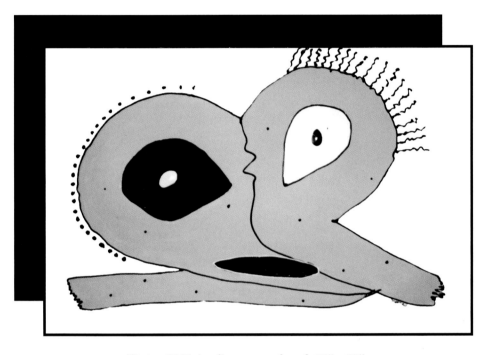

Kissing 2000 Acrylic on water board, 20" x 30"

KISSING

Girls do it…boys do it…

The whole world does it…

Express yourself…feel like…**KISSING??**

MASK II

(Wisdom)

I think before I speak…
I listen, therefore I learn…
I keep both eyes on the world…
There is much to be gained…

Mask II 2000 Acrylic on canvas board, 14" x 18"

MANY ARE BLESSED AND DON'T KNOW IT

Have you heard the story about the man who

Had five cars but no legs…that reminds me..

I have to walk to the store later…

Did you know a man who couldn't see

Went on a tour to see the world?

By the way, there's a strange colored

Bird perched in a nest…

Hey, Mr., Mr., oh yeah he's the man

That can't hear. Have you heard the

Newest songs out? They're great aren't they…

I read the paper today, two people paralyzed

From the neck down…could you please scratch

My back I can't reach it, it sure does itch.

MANY ARE BLESSED AND DON'T KNOW IT.

America 2001 Acrylic on canvas, 24" x 30"

AMERICA

America…I speak your name…
A land where blood flowed
To protect and remain free…
America…I speak your name…
The countries pride still
Remains the same…
Heads held high…
Arms stretched…
Waiting to embrace its own…
America I speak your name…
Wild horses were our automobiles…
Now we travel on wheels of steel…
Land of the free…
The land where my heart will forever be…
AMERICA…I speak your name.

FLYING HIGH

As I travel across the skies,

Floating, floating...

I wonder what great hand is holding

Me so high...

I look through my window, I see

Giant cotton balls that are at

Serenity with themselves...not in

Any great hurry to disappear.

Peeking through the clouds below

Are tiny stars, some moving...some blinking,

Some standing still until the dawn.

Many stars around form galaxies

From where I sit...as I sit still

And I'm moving forward I wonder...

Am I flying or is that giant

Hand turning the world before

Me? Well the fasten seat belt

Sign is back on...I'll have to

Catch up with the stars again later...

I get off in Atlanta...I'm **FLYING HIGH.**

My Private Oasis 2001 Acrylic and sand on canvas, 36" x 48"

MY PRIVATE OASIS

All is quiet and calm…

Serenity surrounds me…

Listen and you too will feel the sounds of…

The ripples in the waters edge…

I can sometimes look…

And feel the water, over my body…

I quietly drift off…while I look at…

MY PRIVATE OASIS.

A LIE IS FASTER THAN THE TRUTH

There are times in a person's life

When reality is questioned…

What is truth and what is a lie?

People imagine lies for truth to

Bring about what they may at

The time wish for, or what

At the time can't be…

A lie is faster than the truth…

A lie can burn your moral house

And scorch your true beliefs,

Your dreams can become true

Instantaneously or at the time of need.

A lie is faster than the truth…

The truth remains waiting to be

Rebuilt because it was lost in

The fire, but refuses to die even though…

A LIE IS FASTER THAN THE TRUTH.

Volcano 2001 Acrylic on water paper, 12" x 13"

VOLCANO

At times my thoughts…
Ooh how deep they run…
My dreams and aspirations…
I yearn to fulfill…the hours in the day…
Not quite enough…
My thoughts…my hand nor pen can accommodate…
My adrenaline now ever flows…
Many of the things I want to share
With those who have two ears…
I take a deep breath…then I continue…
Deep inside…many things
I want not to hide…
Often times I feels like a…**VOLCANO!**

OLD FASHIONED FRIENDS

Our door to our home and hearts with many memories
And cherished meanings, opened swiftly to greet them.
Old fashioned friends are hard to come by…
We've kept close to ourselves, my wife and I,
As we keep a watchful eye over each other.
We keep unwanted people, mere passersby,
Disguised as friend's at bay…
Old fashioned friends are hard to come by…
The introduction was fast, the meeting was slow,
For our guard and their walls were up with search lights,
Wishing and searching to find a friend.
Old fashioned friends are hard to come by…
My wife prepared a meal for two couples,
Putting a special touch that came from the heart
That was shared by real friends.
Old fashioned friends are hard to come by…
There was laughter, stories, sharing, caring…
We told both sides of ourselves without feeling
That what was said would be on the front page
Of the Washington Post…
Old fashioned friends are hard to come by…
Now my wife and I will keep a watchful eye
Over our new…**OLD FASHIONED FRIENDS**…
They were hard to come by…

Spin Off 2001 Acrylic on canvas, 20" x 30"

SPIN OFF

My mother…my father…

White…black…

All that's in between…

At times I'm called a chip

Off the old block…

Or the apple that's still near the tree…

Or just a…**SPIN OFF.**

RIGHT OUTSIDE MY DOOR

I have friends who are dear to me…

I feel compassion and by all means I really care.

If my friends needs me, I want to be there,

If my friends fall, I want to help them up.

If they cry, let me wipe the tears away,

So I may replace them with that of my own.

We'll share the same sorrow or happiness.

I have friends…special friends.

I have friends and we have friendships

That will never die.

My friends are near…they are…

RIGHT OUTSIDE MY DOOR.

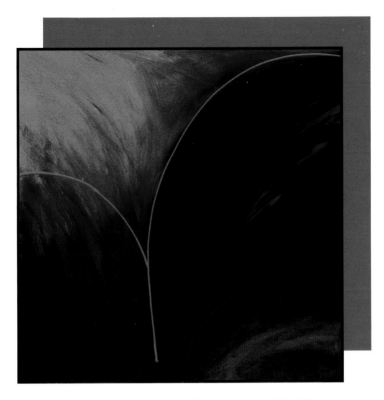

Blooming Orchid 2001 Acrylic on canvas, 32" x 32"

BLOOMING ORCHID

My strengths, I sometimes suppress and hold inside…

My feelings often, I trap and try my best to hide…

Now I have learned…strengths and gifts

Unused may disappear…

Feelings I refuse to reveal,

May never again surface or caress my emotions…

My time is now…while I have time…

I will bloom like the…

BLOOMING ORCHID.

Quotables & Affirmations
By Gerome Meminger Sr.

Quotes to make MY day…make YOUR day
And to lift us up during OUR day.
If the quote fits…say it…

✷ All my limitations are self imposed…I can!

✷ God, what ever you have for me I accept gratefully…
God, what ever I have that you want from me…
I give unselfishly.

✷ Self encouragement doesn't quit until you do.

✷ Successful people do it…
Unsuccessful people wish for it.

✷ Get it right the first time…
The second time will merely be repetitious…

✷ I will not procrastinate…
I'll do something now!

✳ If you have success on your mind and
A deep desire to deliver, you're
What they call...an achiever.

✳ I'll start at the bottom;
I'll work like hell to reach the top...
I will be successful...

✳ Happiness is but a state of mind...my mind states that I can...

✳ I'm happy within myself, now I can be happy with someone else.

✳ At times I'll sit alone... I think to myself...
I'm a dreamer, sometimes I just like being alone...

✳ If I have the will and the desire, then I can have...

✳ Why should I wait...when I can do it myself?

✳ When I hesitate I feel lost so...I'll just do it now...

✳ I'll do the right thing...it's best for me.

* Use your potential to become now!
Tomorrow is today...
Push your damn self!!

* Set goals, not for the effort it takes to
Dream and talk about them,
But to plan and accomplish them.

* First dream, then set your goals...
Then set goals while you keep dreaming.

* Inspire yourself daily, you'll never lose sight.

* When someone doubts your ability,
Become more determined to reach your goals.

* For all the acquaintances I've made, I've gained
Another understanding about life and why I'm living.

* Right or wrong — to agree or disagree it's your option...
For someone else to agree or disagree with you...is theirs.

* Certain favors cost more than the favor cost...

✳ I have high hopes, big dreams and I'm very ambitious...

✳ I'm feeling good about myself today.

✳ I have more inside of me then I realize.
I have a lot to offer
The problem is finding who deserves me.

✳ God does things for a reason...
Your objective as a human being is to....
Reason it out...

✳ When you give your all...
Success will come in return...

✳ Being humble is no cause for shame...
It let's other know you have a good spirit...

✳ One can be meek yet...
Remain very strong...

PHONY PEOPLE

They jump up and shuffle, to the tune of Mr. Bo Jangles.
Phony people…
Love to make a fool of themselves…at mostly others expense.
They like to be loud and stand out for fear no one will notice
Them if they sit and wait for the right opportunity…
Phony people…
They take us down while we're struggling
Trying so hard to regain our ground…
Phony people…
They make promises that they know, there's
No way in hell they intend to keep.
They sport a watch that looks like a Rolex,
But if you look closely, it reads "LowLex.
Phony people…
They wear all of this jewelry, gold, diamonds
But in the meantime, they're between jobs…
Phony people…
They love to borrow money on their terms…
Paying you tomorrow…
While there are only seven days in a week,
Tomorrow should be the eighth…
Phony people…
They don't lie, cheat or steal…
They just have good intentions…
They have potential…which really means
They ain't done a damn thing yet…
Phony people…
They love to tell a joke,
Not knowing the joke is on them…
If you don't have it, maybe the time is not right and …
You haven't earned it. Or maybe you just have potential..
PHONY PEOPLE waste our time!

Shades of Gray 2000 Acrylic on water board, 20" x 30"

SHADES OF GRAY

No lies...

No truth...

Somewhere in the middle are...

SHADES OF GRAY.

DANCE CANDLE DANCE

As I sit and stare into the flame of a candle…

I see the stillness of time with a slight jitter…

The flame burns bright and passes on the

Warmth to the one intended…

It can truly hold one's destiny,

If I could only read and interpret the candle's dance.

Dance candle dance…

The colors are of three, each true to its own.

One day I would like to dance beside the candle

And obtain its true meaning, for it holds many secrets of…

Yours…myself…even the secrets of time…

DANCE CANDLE DANCE.

Speak Easy 2001 Acrylic on canvas board, 18" x 24"

SPEAK EASY

I pace my mind…

I control my tongue…

I speak when I have something to say…

When I have the answers to a few questions…

Then I may engage in dialog…

Wise…maybe…

But I always…**SPEAK EASY.**

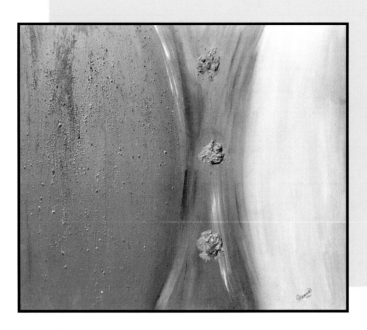

Hour Glass 2001 Acrylic and sand on canvas, 30" x 30"

HOUR GLASS

Tic toc…tic, toc…tic, toc…

Where are those sands of time going?…

Tic, toc…tic, toc…tic, toc…

I look up…it's a quarter past…

Tic, toc…tic, toc…tic, toc…

I look down….

It's two hours and fourteen minutes past my life…

Tic, toc…tic, toc…tic, toc…

The next grain of sand that falls…

I'll hold out my hand and capture one moment

That I will hold dear…

And reset my…

HOUR GLASS.

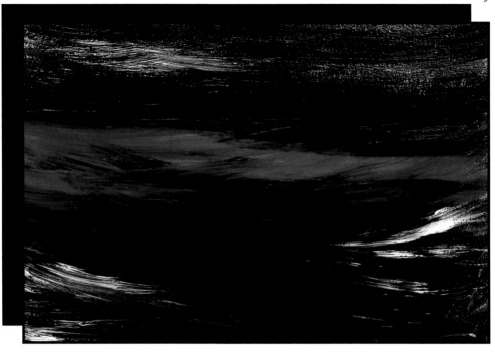

Thunder 2001 Acrylic on water board, 20" x 30"

THUNDER

The calm before the storm…a rocky road…
Hanging ten while trying
To keep your feet planted firmly
On the board atop the waves.
Life brings you ups and downs…
Lemons without sweetener for
The lemonade you will have to make…
Quite often, one might have to try
Several recipes to get the right one.
When things begin to rumble and roll…
Remember…the sun will shine eventually
After the…**THUNDER.**

MY HERO

My mind reaches back in time whenever I see small children

With their arms stretched high above their heads,

Reaching for that giant, whom at any minute will bend

Down to pick them up and protect them.

Time has passed although my yesterdays are still

In my memory, the memories of…"My Hero"…

Certain situations spark memories or my youth as my

Father and I talked, laughed, or even when tears rolled

Down my face which he wiped away with a smile.

I wanted to be just like my dad, because he is…"My Hero"…

As he worked on his car, I would grab a tool and

Begin to repair, or do the best I could…

My father was a wise man, he shared his knowledge with

Me and I absorbed as much as my mind could hold.

My father told me to go as far as I could and

From there…I could go further.

I knew my father loved me very much, even though those words

Would get caught in his throat; but his eyes told it all.

I wanted to make my father proud to say that is my son.

*I still say to this day…he is…***MY HERO.***

A SHORT CUT

Often times a short cut is not always

The shortest path to take…

Achieving success requires, a dream, a goal, or desire, while

Making preparations and mapping a plan of arrival…

The successful road is normally the long way,

And the least traveled…

Upon your arrival you can look back at those who…

Chose…**A SHORT CUT.**

WAITING

Patience is a virtue…

In my mind…In my time…In my space…

I am confident that what I set my mind to know,

I set my sights to see…and my subconscious to do…

At any moment it will come true…

Things that hold the most value,

Often takes the most time…

It's time well spent…I am…**WAITING.**

Waiting 2002 Acrylic on canvas, 25" x 30"

ORANGE MOON

Orange moon dancing on the horizon…

As I gaze, time has little meaning…

My thoughts bring about inner peace…

My feeling not vulnerable…

Orange moon, may I have this

Last dance before you

Once again…fall asleep…

My…**ORANGE MOON.**

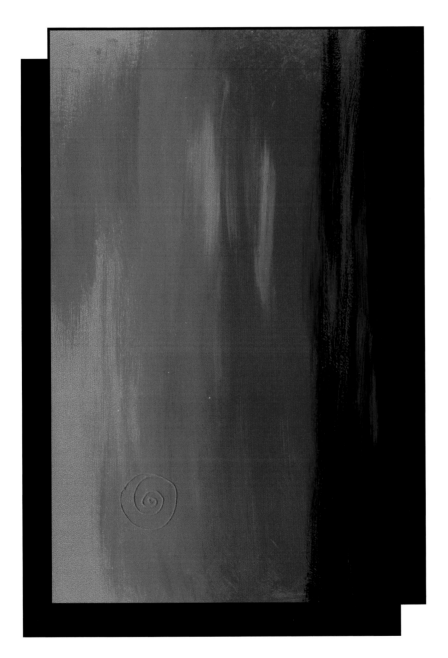

Orange Moon 2001 Acrylic on water board, 20" x 30"

DOES THE SUN SHINE BRIGHTER
ON THE OTHER SIDE?

Suspended, sometimes speechless, often sustained,

Does the sun shine brighter on the other side?

I see clearly, mistakes I've made in the past

And now more than willing to correct.

Had I only known what lies on the other side

And had the courage to change, what I wasn't

At the time, aware of…

Does the sun shine brighter on the other side?…

Today begins anew…times change even a man.

Destiny means more to me than one can imagine…

Time is limited…

Life itself can not be measured.

Suspended, sometimes speechless, often sustained…

If I could reach to see…

DOES THE SUN SHINE BRIGHTER ON THE OTHER SIDE?

Jill and Howard 2001 Acrylic on canvas board, 14" x 18"

JILL AND HOWARD

I see one, I see two…

I see "we"…

I see Jill and Howard,

I see Jill, I see Howard.

I see Jill and Howard…

I see one, I see two, I see three…

I see three?…

I see **JILL AND HOWARD**…

I see a family.

WHO'S KILLING ME NOW?

Yesterday I was red, tomorrow I'll be

White, but today I'm a black man.

Who's killing me now?

I'm dying in these times for

Little or no cause... just because.

I'm hunted, not for my skin or flesh...to be honest,

I really don't know why.

I guess I'm the new game or sport called; "Shoot That Man."

What smiles can be brought about after my death...

What cheers Will be heard?

My mother along with God put me on this earth...

Who made another man the keeper of my life...

Why am I being made an endangered species?

If you think about it one minute, you may realize,

I'm someone's father, a brother, a child or

Maybe just a best friend.

I may be blood of your blood, now appearing in the news...

Oh did I mention in the obituary section...

Who's killing me now?

I want to laugh, cry, sing, dance...

Oh did I mention I'd like to

Live...**WHO'S KILLING ME NOW?**

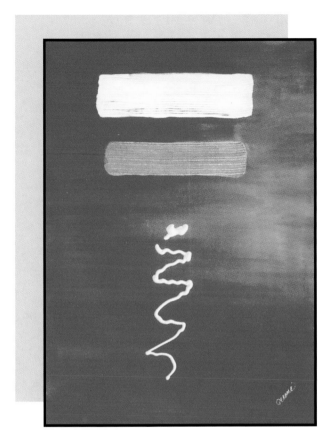

Unraveled 2001 Acrylic on canvas, 25" x 30"

UNRAVELED

Center piece…

Center stone…

Center stage…

At times I like to observe…

I sit and listen…

Wait…and learn…

Haste can often times

Cause your plans to become…

UNRAVELED.

I'M OLD SCHOOL

Old school, that's me, not to be
Confused with old man, or old fool.
I have traveled many roads, several at
One time, on many occasions I had to
Chose very wisely, for some roads have
A point of no return, filled with danger zones.
I listen…I listen…I listen…for mistakes are made,
And I don't have enough life time to make them all,
So…I look, listen and learn, from others mistakes.
I am old school not be confused with old fool.
Old school is always quoting something like:
It's best to be prepared for an opportunity
Because it may only knock once.
Or: people buy what they want and
Beg for what they really need.
Remember the song "Fools Rush In,"
Well, I'll take my time. Old school has a grateful past,
The generation of today should lasso
Many of the dreams that were dreamt…
The cup of knowledge that spilled out was not
An accident, It was shared…old school is a beat, a
Dance, a saying (right on), afros, braids, corn rows,
Bell bottoms, tie dye, Stacy Adam's,
Hot pants (or daisy dukes to some), Chuck Taylor
All Stars, khaki pants, electric slide.
If you take time to feel, then take time to know…
The rest of the story…it's values, dignity, and commitment…
Yeah I'm from the old school, I still pray,
And I play my long playing wax records as I reminisce,
I'M OLD SCHOOL…not to be confused with old fool.

Smoking Sax 2001 Acrylic on canvas board, 16" x 20"

SMOKING SAX

New place, same flavor…the sax,
Drums, bass, piano voices in tune.
New place, same flavor…people
Vibing on the sweet and sour notes
Generated by real people. New place, same flavor…
All come to get a dose, or overdose of live
And in living color sounds…
New place, same flavor…
Red lights low, whispers, claps, applause…
New people, meeting new people.
Hugs, hand shakes, more and more welcomes,
It is about being home. New place…same flavor
Welcome home…**SMOKING SAX.**

I'LL TELL A FRIEND

I have a secret to tell...

However I don't want it to be told...

A friend I could tell...

My secret then would be for them to hold...

Something maybe trivial to some...

Not worth the time to speak...

But when discussed with a friend makes

The cycle complete...

I'LL TELL A FRIEND.

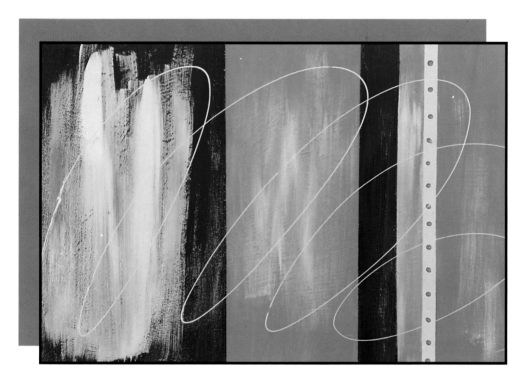

Mermaid 2000 Acrylic on water board, 20" x 30"

MERMAID

Colors deep...

Colors true...

Colors wide and

Clear...lady of the sea

The colors of a **MERMAID.**

MOM'S UNIQUE LOVE

Time has not passed fast enough for me to
Forget things I will always remember…
They mean more now than ever…
Mom's unique love…
I would want, and she would provide,
I'd laugh, she would smile,
I'd cry, she would cradle me, and wipe
Away the tears that rolled down my
Chubby cheeks…Mom's unique love…
A thousand and two questions were asked of Mom daily,
And were answered with the wisdom of experience,
The knowledge of a professor, and the skill of a craftsman…
Mom's unique love…
I'm an adult now, I was taught quite well,
I even remember some or most of my favorite recipes
Which were prepared by the best…Mom.
The taste of mom's cooking is still lingering on my taste buds.
At times I wonder what my mother is doing…I'd ask myself;
Now what would she say for this?
My mother is there no matter where,
She's the first lady in my life,
For she gave me life. I will forever love respect…
Honor…and obey her,
Mom's unique love…
I know I'll never be able to repay
My mother for all that she has done.
Her reward is for me to make her proud…
Mine is to hear her say…that's my child…
MOM'S UNIQUE LOVE.

20/20 2000 Acrylic on canvas, 24" x 30"

20/20

I could sit and stare…
And stare…
And stare…
Wait a minute…
Let me put on my glasses
To help me put my life
Back in focus…
I get one round, so…
I need to see
What I'm doing.
I need to see myself
In…**20/20.**

QUIET STORM

All is calm…

Taking a stroll has crossed my mind…

A small sigh of relief,

For what could have been, but now is…

It is a beautiful setting…

One of the many joys of life's greatest

Wonders to rest your eyes on…

Take your time…lasso the moment…

A time to reflect during the…

QUIET STORM.

Quiet Storm 2000 Acrylic on water board, 20" x 30"

Black Rose 2001 Acrylic and mesh on water board, 20" x 30"

BLACK ROSE

Smell the red, smell the yellow…

Now smell the black.

This rose will never change…

Never grow faint…

It will never wither…

No colors to fade…

Its beauty is as before…

Unchanged…I give to you…

A…**BLACK ROSE.**

Entangled 2002 Acrylic on canvas board, 14" x 18"

ENTANGLED

Lying here...my thoughts are racing,
At speeds my mind is trying to keep up with...
Sometimes life deals you a hand
That you have to study
And remain focused
To truly see...
The real meaning of what
Is actually taking place...
Maybe not in your time...
But...in time...keep the faith, and you
Won't remain...**ENTANGLED.**

Transparent Boxes 2002 Acrylic on canvas, 20" x 30"

TRANSPARENT BOXES

Mind strong...
Boxes deep and plenty...
Several boxes in ones mind...
Vast amount of knowledge stored
In each container...
Decisions...decisions...decisions...
Yet...several solutions...
The mind has the key to unlock the
Doors of technology...and several thereafter...
We communicate to understand...
To grow...to gain knowledge...
Open the boxes of your mind...
The box of wisdom...
The box of knowledge...
The box with courage to continue...
The box that leads you to the next frontier...
Open those...**TRANSPARENT BOXES.**

Two Heads 2002 Acrylic on water paper, 15" x 15"

TWO HEADS

To have an idea…a problem..or a goal…

When discussed by one leaves one opinion…

One feeling, one solution…when discussed by two

Gives two views…times two voices,

Times two solutions to achieve one goal…

That is best solved by…**TWO HEADS.**

IT'S ALRIGHT

You don't always have to be right,

For things to be alright...

You're a mother or a father,

Who wants to have all the answers

To your child's questions to be right...

But you can't help if you don't know everything...

You feel you should because your child

Comes to you for advise...

Give the best answers you can...

Then...if you gave your best...

IT'S ALRIGHT.

Rock 2002 Acrylic and sand on canvas, 22" x 30"

ROCK

I keep my mind sharp…

My body alert, toned and solid…

I struggle and succeed to succeed another day…

I'll go through walls to pursue my dreams…

If it's in my mind it's just a matter of time…

Before I become solid as…a…**ROCK.**

Continuation 2001 Acrylic and sand on canvas, 24" x 30"

CONTINUATION

I started…

I stopped…

Things happened…

Sometimes beyond my control.

I'll get things back together…

Living life is sometimes a…

CONTINUATION.

Dreamer 2001 Acrylic on canvas, 22" x 28"

DREAMER

Sleep, sleep, what a deep sleep…

My hopes I can see…

My desire is right outside my door…

I'm reaching with my right arm, then my left…

At last with both stretched out, locked at the joints…

My dreams are now within reach…keep reaching…

You know dreamer, your dreams are dreams most of the time

Only you can see…stay focused, eyes closed tight…

Mind wide open…and **DREAMER**…dream on.

WAKE UP YOU

I'm here…you're there…

You're not touching me like you once would…

The soft tones in your voice have grown deeper…

I'm here…you're there…our conversations are short…

They seldom end with a smile…it seems our mental channels are

Constantly changing…turning to another frequency…

The conversations are getting crossed…

Often times than not…the tv set is looking different…

Do we now watch a different program at the same time…

It's past midnight…the hum is all that's left on the screen…

It's time to…**WAKE UP YOU.**

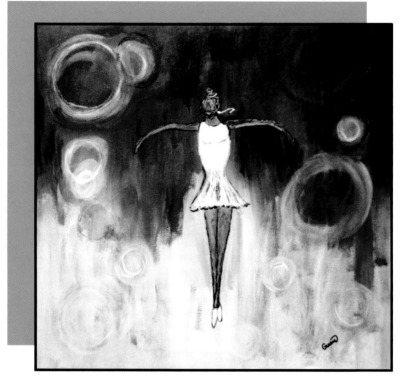

Bubbles and Ballet 2002 Acrylic on canvas, 30" x 30"

BUBBLES AND BALLET

My dream is to dance...

To be very light on my feet...

Stand on my toes...until my spins and turns are complete.

I want to float through the air ...with the greatest of ease...

Dance...with a smile...as graceful as I please...

I want to feel like the colors of magenta,

With a splash of purple and mauve at my side...

I will rise...and my body will sway...with my fantasy of...

BUBBLES AND BALLET.

BEST EFFORT

I tried to do something…

It did not work the

Way I planned…

I tried a different approach…

It did not work the

Way I planned…

Decision time…

Do I give up?…

Do I retreat?…

If it is meant for me,

It will be…

I'll try again tomorrow and…

The day after…

*I'll give it my…***BEST EFFORT.**

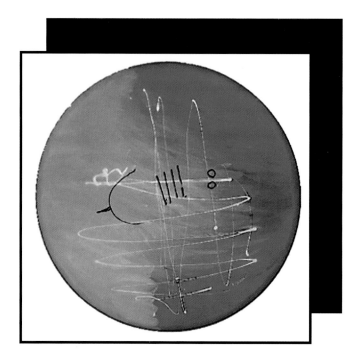

Violin 2001 Acrylic on canvas, 36"

VIOLIN

I'll play a song…

I'll play a sweet, and ooh so high a note…

The note that will make me…

Float through my day…

And not want to rest…

Even when I may weary…

Today is a day…

Special to me indeed…

Today I know exactly what I need…

Today…I'll play my sweet…

VIOLIN.

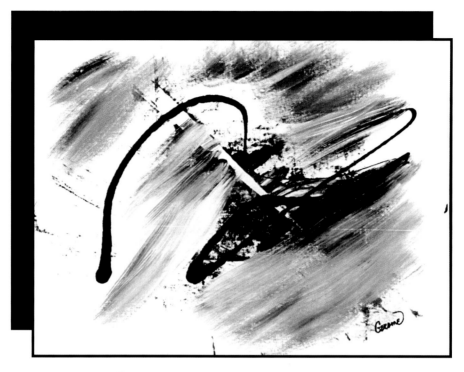

Tell Tale 2001 Acrylic on canvas board, 16" x 20"

TELL TALE

Within you lies
Destiny, hope and
Maybe a dream…
A glimpse of me
Will take you on a
Journey to your desired
Never, never land.
Take a moment and
Let's…
TELL *a* **TALE**.

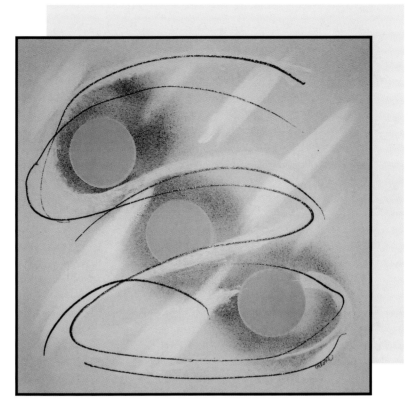

Strawberries And Dreams 2002 Acrylic on canvas board, 32" x 32"

STRAWBERRIES AND DREAMS

Silver moon...purple moon...
My strawberry moon...
Is it possible for man to fly...on his own?...
Answer...yes...
The mind may become the vehicle to deliver such
A wonderful flight...batteries not included...
The mind has a resource of untapped energy...
Energy because it comes from within...
Live your life and experience your pleasures...
Sleep now...and have sweet...
STRAWBERRIES AND DREAMS.

Rise 2001 Acrylic on canvas, 36" x 48"

RISE

Today is a day, is a day…

No…today is my day…

Today I'll smell the ocean…

Today I'll sniff the breeze…

I'll inhale then exhale life…

And…my pursuit of happiness…

Today…I'll…**RISE.**

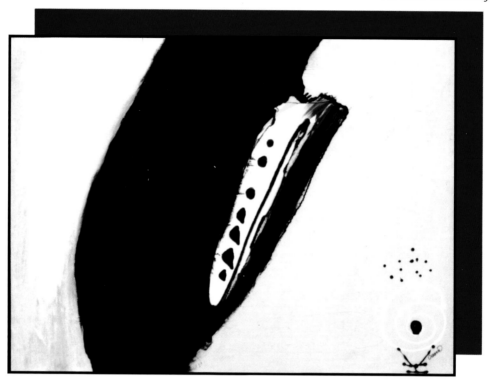

A Formal Affair 2001 Acrylic on canvas, 36" x 48"

A FORMAL AFFAIR

Greetings, greetings, and salutations...

Wine and dine, and dine again...

I'm the host...

Sometimes your wish may be my command...

At times I my wear jeans or shorts...

But today I feel like a tux...

Lets make this...

A FORMAL AFFAIR.

Cocktails For Two 2002 Acrylic on canvas board, 16" x 20"

COCKTAILS FOR TWO

It's my pleasure…staring in your eyes…
Looking at your smile, as we laugh together…
I'll impress you yet…
When we are engaged in conversation,
I see a warm glow about you…
Your lips look sweet and as soft as any virgin cotton…
I yearn for the moment when my lips
Join yours to form a perfect union…
The sparkles will truly rejoice as they shine ever so bright…
Thanks for the hours…may they turn into days…
Months…years…a life time…
For this is the first of many…
COCKTAILS FOR TWO.

Café Latté 2001 Acrylic and sand on water board, 20" x 30"

MY FRIEND, ME AND A CUP OF TEA

Well here we are again…time I guess Is aware of our presence
Because it seems to speed up once we're together.
We talk, sip on our cups of tea,
Just my friend, me and our cups of tea…
It's quite relaxing being able to share thoughts
We held in our head all day that were just anxiously
Awaiting to be heard in the company of….
My friend, me and our cups of tea…
Nothing has to be important in our conversation,
Or nothing can ever be taken too lightly…for we are in
Tune to what is being said and hear what
Is being told…it's special just…
MY FRIEND, ME AND OUR CUPS OF TEA.

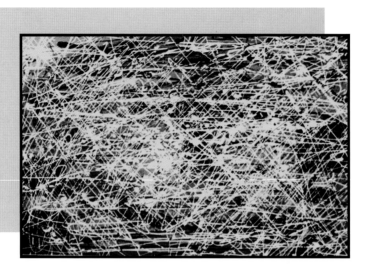

Five Secret Boxes 2002 Acrylic on canvas board, 24" x 30"

FIVE SECRET BOXES

What's mine is yours…

What's yours is mine…secrets not included…

My personality, my attitude, my method of coping…

Some secrets I'll share, although some I don't dare…

You know my favorites…you know my likes and dislikes…

You know my secret hiding place…you know enough…

So…I'll keep the rest to myself…to remain me…

We're not joined at the hip…we are individuals…

Never to be confused with possessions…

We each are entitled to…**FIVE SECRET BOXES.**

A Full Circle 2001 Acrylic on canvas, 36" x 48"

A FULL CIRCLE

Generation after generation…
Come see..learn…exchange ideas…
Learn by listening…
Because you will hear and see…
Certain things again…
Here today…gone tomorrow…
Back the next day…
History has a way of repeating itself…
Life comes around in…
A FULL CIRCLE.

MY WORDS MAYBE NOT

Speak my words…

They hold many a truth…

Life is not a game and I've lost my youth…

Things are done, things are told…

My words have a story…

Shared by some…

Ignored by the remaining few…

The words I share…I shan't lie…

Many I have not the answer for…

Maybe they come from on high…

The words I won't question…I'll just keep pen in hand…

In hopes of writing my ticket into…what's promised land…

My words maybe…

MY WORDS MAYBE NOT…

GEROME

I'm told I have a gift, I'm told I'm an artist...

I'm told my art can spread joy and bring

Pleasure through my work...

When I paint, I paint freely...

When I write poetry, I stay true to myself...

I'll let God tell me the rest of my story...

I'm...**GEROME.**